ELECTRONICS

ELECTRONICS

JoAnn Chirico, Ph.D.

VGM Career Horizons
a division of NTC Publishing Group
Lincolnwood, Illinois USA

Photo Credits:
Pages 1, 15, 29, 43, and 57: Photo Network, Tustin, CA; page 71:
Cessna Aircraft Company, Wichita, KS.
All other photographs courtesy of the author.

Library of Congress Cataloging-in-Publication Data

Chirico, JoAnn.
     Electronics / JoAnn Chirico.
        p.   cm. — (VGM's career portraits)
     Includes index.
     Summary: Presents information on career possibilities in
electronics and electricity. Includes suggested activities for
finding out more about a specific career.
     ISBN 0-8442-4373-6 (hardback)
     1. Electronics—Vocational guidance—Juvenile literature.
2. Electric engineering—Vocational guidance—Juvenile literature.
[1. Electronics—Vocational guidance. 2. Electric engineering—
Vocational guidance. 3. Vocational guidance.] I. Title.
II. Series.
TK7820.C53 1995   95-18548
621.3'023—dc20   CIP
                                                  AC

Published by VGM Career Horizons, a division of NTC Publishing Group
4255 West Touhy Avenue
Lincolnwood (Chicago), Illinois 60646-1975, U.S.A.
© 1996 by NTC Publishing Group. All rights reserved.

5 6 7 8 9 0 QB 9 8 7 6 5 4 3 2 1

Contents

I'm ten years old. . . .
TV is my life.

Kevin, *Home Alone II*

Dedication

To my parents, Mary and Joseph Chirico.

Introduction

Electronics has revolutionized life. Electronics is small, fast, and smart. It saves lives in hospitals. Electronic robots save us work. Electronics guides us around the world and to the moon. Electronics is about information. It is information received, transmitted, and responded to. This information feedback process is called *cybernetics*.

Electricity and electronics touch èvery aspect of our lives. From aviation to zoology, electronics is involved. It even entertains us. Some major job categories are discussed in this book. The jobs in each of these areas center on similar types of work.

Creating. Having a good idea and bringing an idea to life is the job of the design team. The team is made up of engineers, assisted by technicians, who use their knowledge of electric circuits to solve a problem or find better and better ways to satisfy human needs.

Producing. Finding the best methods and materials to build the product is another engineering task. Constructing a high-quality product efficiently on the plant floor is the responsibility of the production supervisors and assembly workers.

Installing, Operating, and Maintaining. Skilled technicians usually have responsibility for installing, servicing, and repairing electronics. Except for consumer products, most electronics need to be operated by trained technicians.

Marketing and Selling. Finding people who can benefit from a company's products or finding a new use for a product is called marketing. Depending on how sophisticated the product is, these jobs may require engineering degrees, business degrees, or both. Some areas of consumer electronics may require high school degrees with on-the-job training or two-year technical degrees.

Communicating. User manuals and press releases have to bridge the gap between technical language and popular language. Most companies have writers on staff to do this. Skill in communication as well as technological knowledge are needed. This may be a writer who is technologically gifted or a technician or engineer who has also developed communication skills.

On any one project, people from each of these areas will work together as a team. The team will use the best ideas from each of the specialties.

ELECTRONICS

IN

POWER PLANTS

ZAP! Imagine life without electricity. It's impossible. It's all around us—in a lightning bolt, a watch or calculator, even in the beating of our hearts. Electric utility plants generate electricity from an energy source, harness it as current, and send it to homes, businesses, and industries. Some of the energy sources are renewable: some are nonrenewable. The renewable sources are those that are regularly replenished. We can't use them up. These are sources

like the wind, falling water (hydro), heat from deep in
the earth or a hot spring (geothermal, although some
scientists exclude this from the renewable list), quickly
grown plant sources (biomass), and the sun (solar or
photovoltaic). Nonrenewable are those that we can use
up faster than they are replaced by nature. These are
the fossil fuels like coal, gas, and oil. Nuclear fuels, like
plutonium are used in very small quantities.

Transforming energy to power involves three giant
steps:

1. Finding a plentiful source of energy,

2. Converting the energy to a usable form, and

3. Delivering it to the places where it will be used.

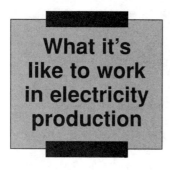

**What it's
like to work
in electricity
production**

The jobs that are required to produce electricity vary in the amount
of education required, the working
conditions encountered, and the
salary it is possible to make.

The physical environment of
workers in the utility industry
varies greatly. A technician might
be outside repairing lines in
freezing weather or baking in the
sun. Engineers travel everywhere
in the world surveying the land-
scape where new lines will be laid
or new power sources cultivated.
Operators burning coal will have
a much dirtier, less pleasant
environment than operators using
falling water as a source of
energy. Inside the power plants,
the conditions are clean and
pleasant. The potential of danger
from radiation to workers and the

environment surrounding atomic plants are well documented and constantly monitored.

Let's find out what happens on the job

Research engineers find new sources of energy or make more efficient use of current resources. They develop safer, more efficient machinery to generate and transform electricity. Skilled technicians help the engineers draft plans, build and test model equipment, monitor research results, and monitor operations in plants.

Energy management staff find the best ways for customers to use electrical power and also suggest ways to conserve it. They come up with new ideas, like the "cool" lightbulb, that help solve energy problems. They can have technical or business backgrounds or both.

Technicians and operators in the control room generate electricity from the energy source. Whether a plant uses fossil fuels or atomic power, it uses energy to boil water and produce steam, which turns turbines to generate low-voltage electric current. Other energy sources may create mechanical power directly from their activity. Operators also maintain and repair the power plant machinery. Transmission and dispatch workers insure that the current flows through the lines that comprise the grid at voltages sufficient to meet demands from various parts of the service area.

Line crews and electricians install and repair the lines that transmit the current from the plant to the homes and industries where it is used. In addition to the technical positions, the utility industry is supported by a large staff of managers, financial officers, customer service, and clerical help.

The future of electronics in power plants

The electric utilities and industries will continue to look for safer, cleaner, efficient, and more cost effective ways of generating electricity. They are also finding new customers and new uses for electricity. Demand for engineers, technical workers should continue well into the next century.

The rewards, the pay, and the perks

Keeping up with technology encourages utilities to offer on-the-job-training and other educational opportunities for its employees. Advancement into jobs with more responsibility requires excellent on-the-job performance and a willingness to learn new skills. It may take from 4 to 8 years to reach the highest levels in any one job category, such as electrician, dispatcher, or equipment operator.

What all the jobs have in common is challenge. The challenge is to invent new technologies to use electricity in more powerful and efficient ways or to develop skills in using the new technologies and equipment as they are invented.

Getting started

A high school diploma is the key to entry-level positions. Employers provide on-the-job training to move from apprentice to higher positions. But, vocational school training can help get a job and advance more quickly in your job. Working on the power lines requires physical stamina and good health. These jobs often require a commercial driver's license because of the large trucks used on the job in repair and maintenance.

Entering the research field as a technician requires a technical school education or a college engineering degree.

Let's Meet...

Art Lilley
Energy Engineer

Art helps communities find their best energy resources. His specialty is remote areas anywhere in the world; atop mountains, in jungles, in deserts, or on islands. He is an expert in renewable energy resources.

What first interested you in this field?

About 2 billion people in the world don't have electricity. We know that having electricity can improve lives dramatically. Bringing them affordable electricity is a challenge and an opportunity to really make an important difference in the world. I work with all the renewable resources, but I chose photovoltaics as a specialty. We know how to implement it on a villagewide, or citywide basis, and because it is a passive system with no moving parts, it is easily maintained in remote parts of the world.

What kind of special training or background do you need?

I have engineering and business degrees and experience. Working in manufacturing, I learned the importance of understanding what customers want. Technical knowledge is necessary to know what is possible and how to accomplish it cost effectively. I really use my background in

strategic planning to imagine and work toward a desirable future. You have to develop the product and the customers or market for the product together, in a step-by-step way that makes sense.

What are your favorite activities on your job?

I love traveling all over the world to find communities that we can help. I like helping them define their needs and the best way to satisfy them. This takes a lot of creative problem solving. Then I enjoy writing the proposals to convince industries and governments to support the projects.

What are the most rewarding aspects of your job?

Visiting the communities after power has been established and witnessing the impact on people's lives is most rewarding. One example is a man who had to live away from his family because he needed refrigeration for the fish that he caught. He had to live in another town, do business there, and send money home. Now he lives with his family and operates his business in the village.

What accomplishment are you most proud of?

We have just received a contract to electrify 100 villages in Indonesia, which is a chain of islands. We will electrify village by village, but as the system grows, we'll begin connecting them into a network. This is one of the first large demonstrations of a new model for electrification.

Community Energy Survey

Become an energy detective in your own community. Call your local electric utility, municipal government, and local weather services to find the answers to these questions.

What energy source does your electric utility company use to generate electricity?

Is this a renewable or nonrenewable resource?

Are there secondary or backup systems of energy production available?

What renewable resources are available in your area?
- How many days of full sunlight per year are there?
- Can you find a month-by-month average?
- What are the average wind speeds per month?
- Is there a source of steadily falling water?
- Are there roadside or river lights that are solar powered?
- How many uses of solar power can you find in your home?
- In your community?
- Does anyone in your class have fully or partially powered solar homes?

Let's Meet...

Karen Kiger
Transmission and Dispatch Supervisor

Karen works for an electric utility company. She ensures a steady flow of electricity along 12,000-volt lines and equipment. She schedules regular maintenance and solves problems when service is disrupted.

How did you start out in this field?

West Penn Power advertised an electrician training program. I enjoyed the training and was hired as an apprentice 6 months later. I loved being outside, working with tools, figuring out what was wrong with equipment, and fixing it. I worked my way up to Electrician Class A, the highest level.

Did you need any other training to move into the job that you have now?

Most of the training is on-the-job training. I take extra courses so that my opportunities aren't limited. After 10 years, I moved inside as a transmission and dispatch (T&D) technician. Working as an electrician was good preparation for T&D because I already knew what goes wrong with the lines and equipment and what needs to be done to repair them.

What do you like most about your job?

The job is different every single day. I enjoy that. You never know what will happen next. It could be very quiet while you schedule opening and closing lines and crews for routine maintenance work. Then, as quickly as a thunderstorm can hit, it gets hectic and rushed, with loads of problems to solve. You might need to be switching equipment on and off, identifying problems and dispatching crews to several places all at once.

Are there any aspects of the job that you don't like?

When power goes out, people want to know when it will be restored. They call and are very anxious to know when their electricity will be on. Most times they have important reasons for wanting to know. They may have to ask their workers to go home or to cancel the next shift. Until I know where the problem is and what it is, I can't help them. It's very frustrating for me, not to have the information they need and frustrating for them if they don't understand why I don't know.

What will be your next career move?

Becoming a shift supervisor would be the next step up the ladder. These supervisors monitor and regulate the highest voltage lines. It's not likely that I'll move into one of these positions because in this particular company, the current supervisors are all about my age. Unless someone moves, there won't be any openings.

What Happens during a "Brownout" or Power Outage?

Problem:

Uh-oh. Your favorite program is on and the screen flickers. The clock on the VCR starts to flash. The lights dim and then go bright again. You have just experienced a power "brownout." But, what's happened to the power lines? Why did you lose power and then regain it?

Answer:

- Something is caught on the line. Perhaps it's a tree limb or an animal. An automatic **recloser** turns the power off for a second to give the branch or animal a chance to blow off or get free. Most companies have their reclosers set to give three chances for the line to be clear. If it doesn't clear by the third try, the power will shut off until the line is repaired.

- An extra load was put on your power supply. One of your appliances may have just started. A refrigerator, microwave, air conditioner, or other motorized appliance can cause a fluctuation in power.

- A loose connection, or an old, dirty, or corroded plug may be the culprit. This may cause a "short" in your home that causes a voltage fluctuation.

Success Stories

Magma Power Company Magma Power is a mid-sized company that generates electricity from geothermal resources, using the heat of the earth. It operates seven geothermal plants in California and Nevada. It sells the electricity it produces to Southern California Edison, one of the largest electric utilities in the United States. Magma Power has clearly shown that renewable resources can produce significant amounts of electricity at reasonable costs.

Maria Telkes Maria Telkes, physical chemist and solar energy expert, devoted most of her career to developing and applying solar energy technology. Her list of accomplishments and awards was very long by the time she retired at the age of 78. She developed the technology for the first solar-powered home in Dover, Massachusetts, in 1948. She invented a still for life rafts that could convert seawater into fresh water, using solar energy. This system was enlarged for land use on the Virgin Islands. Her inventions were used in the Polaris undersea missions and the Apollo space missions. She received many awards and honors. Among the awards she received were the Society of Women Engineers Achievement Award, The International Solar Engineering Society (American Section, Charles Greely Abbot) Award and was honored for her contributions by the National Academy of Science Building Advisory Board.

Find Out More

You and power

The customer service department of an electric utility can arrange for speakers to come to your school and even provide tours of its plant. Their phone number is listed on your electric bill.

Your electric bill contains a lot of information. It tells you how much electricity was used during the last month and how much it cost. Some utility companies also tell how much you used during the same time last year.

Survey your class to determine their electricity usage.

- Compare families' usage according to the size of the family
- Compare according to the number of major electric appliances they have such as oven, clothes dryer, and furnace.

Does everyone have the same electric company? If not, compare the price of electricity charged by the different companies.

Find out more about power

To learn more about power, you can write to:

American Solar Energy Society
2400 Central Ave.
Boulder, CO 80301

Manager of Educational Services
Edison Electric Institute
1111 19th St., N.W.
Washington, DC 20036

National Photovoltaics Program
U.S. Department of Energy
National Renewable Energy Lab
Golden, CO 80401-3391

Solar Energy Industries
    Association
777 N. Capitol St., N.E.
Washington, DC 22202

Renew America
1400 16th St., N.W., Suite 710
Washington, DC 20036

ELECTRONICS IN MEDICINE

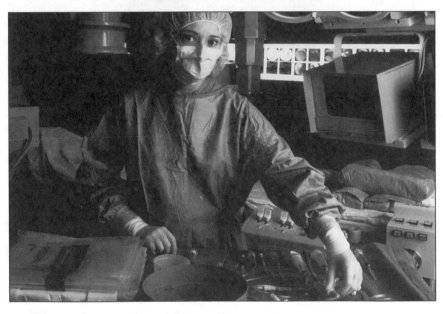

Electronic equipment used in medicine is called bio-medical equipment. Heart and lung machines, pace-makers, and kidney dialysis machines fill in for body organs that are failing. Through bionics, artificial limbs can work with the body's electric current just as natural limbs do. From an idea to solve a problem, through the design and production of the electronics, to its use with the people who need it, a skilled team of dedicated people keep us all our healthiest, through electronic wizardry.

The importance of electronics in medicine

In a hospital, a biomedical equipment technician repairs and maintains the electronic machinery on which so many lives depend. Each machine has to work accurately and effectively. There is no room for mistakes.

There are many kinds of biomedical equipment. Diagnostic and monitoring equipment help doctors and nurses find out what is wrong with a patient and watch for signs of progress or trouble. It includes machines like the electrocardiogram and electroencephalograph that monitor and measure heart impulses and brain waves. Ultrasound viewing and X-ray and CAT scans lets doctors see inside patients without cutting them open.

Some equipment is used for treating patients. It might correct or help perform vital functions. Ventilators keep a patient breathing regularly. Hearing aids enhance sound vibrations to the inner ear. Kidney dialysis machines and pacemakers can take over some bodily functions. Defibrillators, which we've all seen on TV, are used to restore a steady heartbeat. Physical therapists use ultrasonic vibrations in treating muscles. Electronic pumps deliver food or medicine to patients in measured doses, just as they need it.

Hospital labs are filled with electronic devices. Centrifuges, coagulators, cell washers, and microscopes are a few. The operating room has perhaps the most of all.

Let's find out what happens on the job

Careers in biomedical electronics blend working with people and working with technology. You can enter the field in many ways. Each requires different sets of skills, a different level or type of education. Let's follow an electronic device from its birth as an idea to its use to outline the career possibilities.

- Product developers get the ideas for new equipment. They could have a business or technical background or both. They meet with people in the medical field to find out what problems they have and what kind of equipment they need to solve it.

- Engineering managers figure out whether or not their company could create a product to meet the physician's or hospital's needs.

- Design engineers create the electronic circuitry and "invent" the machine. Along with industrial engineers, they work out all the details of the product and how to make it in a factory.

- Electronics technicians work with the engineers every step of the way. They carry out the plans of the engineers.

Surgical technicians, medical technologists, and biomedical technicians operate and repair most of the equipment in a hospital or doctor's office. They may also work for research and pharmaceutical companies or government health agencies.

What it's like working with electronics in medicine

The two main features of all these jobs are:

1. The reward of knowing that your work saves lives and improves people's health. This is a huge responsibility that motivates everyone to do their best.

2. The challenge of keeping up with the new technology. It is an expanding field and there are always new products to be thought of, developed, built, and used. Everyone in the field is a lifelong learner.

If you love people and technology, if you like challenges, this is an area for you to consider.

The rewards, the pay, and the perks

The biomedical field has many perks. Because you have to keep up with technology, many corporations and hospitals will help you continue your education. They may pay for you to take courses that keep you up-to-date. They may increase your salary as you increase your knowledge.

The working environment is pleasant. Because of the nature of the work, it must be clean. There are some health hazards if you are working with the equipment that causes radiation. Here, you work protected by lead vests, and your exposure is measured constantly by a special pin worn on your uniform.

The pay scale depends on your level of training, and is generally quite good.

Getting started

Most of the jobs in biomedical electronics require a 2-year degree. This training qualifies you for a job as a technician. Some 2-year degrees, such as electronics technician, give you the technology dimension. Others, like surgical technician or biomedical electronics technician, add the people or medical dimension.

A college degree in engineering is necessary to design equipment. Specialized training in biomedicine in addition to engineering is helpful. A business or engineering degree is necessary to enter product development.

Climbing the career ladder

Technicians' salaries increase as they get more years of experience. They may begin to supervise or train other technicians. Engineers also advance by increasing their responsibility for larger projects. They might move into management and supervise other engineers to raise their salaries.

Let's Meet...

Bruce Kirin
Electronic Circuit Designer

Bruce has had a long career in electronics. Now, he is busy designing electronic circuitry to work in ventilators that monitor a person's breathing and correct breathing problems that arise.

How did you become interested in electronics?

I have always been interested in how things worked. I was lucky that my parents allowed me to take apart almost anything in the house, as long as I promised to put it back together. I was also lucky to live near a dump. There you have an endless supply of things that you can take apart and never have to put back together!

Aside from your education and experience, what personal qualities make you successful in your design job?

Some of the qualities are things that are important in a lot of jobs: attention to detail and liking math and science. There is also a creative element in design electronics. Being able to come up with a circuit that can do something that hasn't been done before is creative.

What do you like most about your job?

There are two things. First, it is really exciting to take an idea and see it become an actual product. Second is knowing that someone is using a product you designed and that it is making their life better. That is really rewarding.

What are your least favorite activities on the job?

After the design is completed, there is a very long process necessary to make it a product. This involves a lot of paperwork. Then, there are tests that mean more paperwork. It is not one of the parts of the job that I like.

How was your first day on the job?

Three things happened right in a row when I began working. First, I was thrilled that for the first time in my life, I had all the supplies to build whatever I needed. Second, I was terrified of being responsible for the success of a project. Third, I was relieved to find out that I was working on a team, that my ideas would be critiqued and reviewed and that there were people who I could turn to for help. In school you are expected to do everything on your own. At work, you have to be able to get things done as part of a team.

Building an Electronic Circuit

Bruce designs electronic circuits. A circuit is a pathway for electric current. The wiring in your house forms an electric circuit. Electronic circuits are different. They have components that control the small current and make it do very precise and sophisticated jobs. Electronic circuits are built on circuit boards, using the components pictured below, or on chips that use chemicals to do the jobs of the components.

Main Components in a Circuit Board

Active Components & Symbols		Passive Components & Symbols		Miscellaneous & Symbols	
Diode	⊣►⊢	Resistor	/\/\/\	Switch	—o⌐
Transistor	—Ⓧ	Capacitor	⁺⊤⊥	Wire	—
Battery or voltage source	AC DC Ⓧ ⊥B+	Inductor	⌒⌒⌒	Bulb	⊚
Light Emitting diode (LED)	⊕►				

The board to which the components are attached is called a *breadboard.* It contains strips of copper that are connected by the components, according to the engineer's design, to form the circuit.

Here is a schematic of a circuit as an engineer would draw it. It uses symbols for each component.

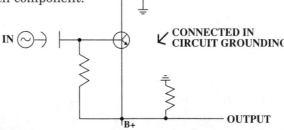

The picture shows you what a completed circuit looks like.

You can build a simple circuit using a battery, thin gauge copper wire, and a small light bulb. The circuit is open at the "switch." Test several materials at the switch to see which will act as conductors in the circuit, closing it to light the bulb. See which will act as insulators.

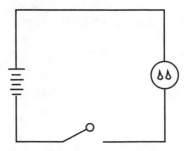

Let's Meet...

Bonnie Reid
Surgical Technician or "Scrub Nurse"

Bonnie is a registered nurse who works in the operating room. She has to know what electronic equipment surgeons will need, almost before they do, get it ready for them, and put it into their hand just as they go to use it.

What has been your career path and what special training did you need along the way?

I began as a nurse's aide. This required a training program and license. As my family grew older, I took additional training as a surgical technician. This is a very technical training in the use of the surgical equipment. I spent 4 years as an operating room "scrub nurse." Then, I completed the coursework and became licensed as a registered nurse.

What are the qualities that make you successful in your job?

You must have a sense of humor. The operating room is a very tense, highly stressful place. Laughter brings a sense of calmness and can help the operating team focus and work together better as a team.

You also need a lot of patience. During an operation, tempers can fly. You have to be able to take the stress of the situation and use it

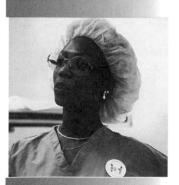

to motivate you, not defeat you. You must
thrive on and love challenges.

Do you have any qualities that you have to "battle" for you to do your job well?

It is hard to be patient while under so much
stress. If a doctor speaks harshly during an
operation, I have to be able to take a moment
to think about the anger I may be feeling
before I react. You also have to be able to
prevent yourself from becoming overwhelmed.
Sometimes the operating room nurses are
expected to know more than they think they
know. You have to have confidence in your
ability to handle whatever arises.

It is very hard to see a patient come back
repeatedly for more and more surgery. In
many chronic cases, you know that there is
not much that you will do except keep them
more comfortable, until the next surgery.

What is your biggest problem in the job?

Staying up-to-date with all the advances is
hard. You have to keep yourself motivated
because you're no longer in school. At night,
I can't just go home and rest. I have to read
articles and learn.

What advice would you give students interested in exploring the field?

Find out information about the field of biomedicine. Don't let the challenges of the
technology scare you. It might seem difficult
at first, but that makes it even more rewarding when you find out you can do it.

Operating Room Electronics

The many electronic tools in the operating room make surgery safer for patients and more effective in healing patients. These tools are handled by skilled technicians, as well as doctors, while surgery progresses. See if you can identify the job that each electronic instrument performs. Match the letter of the instrument with the number of the job listed below.

The Instruments
A.   Endoscope
B.   Laser (includes the electrosurgical unit)
C.   Ventilator
D.   Electronic drill
E.   Defibrillator
F.   Anesthesia
G.   Electrocardiogram
H.   Ultrasound

Here are the jobs that they do
1.   Delivers an electric shock to patient to restore a steady heartbeat.
2.   Uses high-frequency sound waves of great power to replace cutting in a variety of procedures or to view organs without invasive procedures.
3.   Monitors and displays a graph of the patient's heartbeat.
4.   Used to desensitize patients for surgery and to monitor blood chemistry.
5.   Highly precise heat-producing tool with many uses—from making incisions, to closing small blood vessels, to cleaning arteries.
6.   Used to gain entry into hard bone tissue.
7.   A thin tube that uses fiber optics to allow surgeons to look into the body through a tiny incision and view it on a television screen.
8.   Helps patients maintain a regular breathing pattern.

Answers: A-7, B-5, C-8, D-6, E-1, F-4, G-3, H-2.

Success Stories

The Jarvik-7 was the first artificial heart to be transplanted into a patient. It was developed by Robert K. Jarvik and a team of biomedical engineers at the University of Utah. The patient who received the heart, Barney J. Clark, lived for 113 days after the historic operation. The longest a patient has survived with the artificial heart has been about 20 months. The artificial heart is used to keep patients alive while waiting for a human heart transplant.

Martine Kempf invented Katalavox, the voice-command wheelchair. It give mobility and freedom to thousands of people who cannot use their arms to operate a regular wheelchair. Kempf was inspired by the victims of the medication thalidomide. Their mothers had taken the medication while they were pregnant. Their children had a number of birth defects, denying them use of their arms, legs, or both. Some were born without them. Kempf was also inspired by the work of her father. Her father had invented mechanisms for operating the foot pedals of a car with hand controls. His invention gave mobility to thousands of adults who did not have use of their legs.

Find Out More

You and electronics in medicine

The community education or public relations office of most hospitals give tours or provide speakers for schools and youth groups. Tell them that you are interested in the use of biomedical equipment. They are usually happy to help others learn more about their work helping people. Local emergency medical rescue teams are another good source of information.

If you have any broken electronic equipment at home or school, ask if you can have it for experimenting. Take it apart. Does it have a circuit board or chips? If it has a board, some of the components may still work. Can you identify them?

**Find out
more about
electronics
in medicine**

American Medical Technologists
710 Higgins Rd.
Park Ridge, IL 60068

American Society for Medical
    Technology
2021 L St., N.W., Suite 400
Washington, DC 20036

Institute of Electrical and
    Electronics Engineers
345 E. 47th St.
New York, NY 10017

American Nurses Association
2420 Pershing Rd.
Kansas City, MO 64108

American Medical
    Electroencephalographic
    Association
850 Elm Grove Rd.
Elm Grove, WI 53122

ELECTRONICS
IN ROBOTICS AND
MANUFACTURING

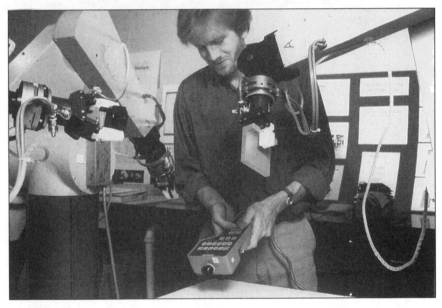

R obots are workers who can do only what they are told to do. They may not think for themselves. They are electronic wonders made of electronic circuitry and mechanical parts. They work without rest, doing the same task hour after hour, day after day, year after year. They can lift more than any human, perform the most delicate tasks with much more precision than humans. But, they haven't replaced human workers. As we'll see, good workers need minds of their own.

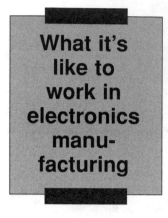

What it's like to work in electronics manufacturing

- Industrial engineers figure out exactly how the product will be assembled, which materials can be used to assemble the product in a way that it can do all that it is supposed to.

- Production managers carry out the engineers' plan on the factory floor. They order and organize the materials for production. They organize the workers into teams to get the job done.

- Production supervisors are the team leaders of the factory workers. He or she helps the team do its best job and make sure that each product assembled meets quality and safety standards.

- Assembly workers put the parts of the product together. Some work in lines, doing a small part of the job, over and over. More often, they work assembling and testing large sections of the product. These larger parts are put together into the final product by another group of workers.

- Robots accomplish their work following the directions of computer programs that control their actions. This makes them different than ordinary machines and different than humans, neither of which are programmed for specific responses. Robots may be very sophisticated, responding differently to different messages from their environment, such as changes in temperature, slowing of the production line, or missing parts.

The pleasures and pressures of the job

Electronics workers have to be very adaptable. The products they assemble change design often to keep up with advances in technology and consumer demands. Companies are getting involved in helping workers learn new skills through formal education and on-the-job training. This applies to all levels of jobs—from assembly to industrial engineering.

A quick survey of your home, school, or local electronics store will show you how much we depend on electronics in our work and for our entertainment. An idea for a new product or improving an old one and the know-how to make it are highly valued and rewarded. There is unlimited opportunity for the clever and creative to develop new electronic products.

The rewards, the pay, and the perks

Companies often pay employees for suggestions to cut the costs of making a product or making a better product. Many will also have profit sharing. Each worker gets more in their paycheck when the company earns more money. Working "smarter" benefits everyone.

Automation and robotics will replace many jobs in production. But, the jobs replaced will be those that are too dangerous or too monotonous for humans. The development of more complex electronics will create more jobs for workers who develop electronics skills, decision-making and problem-solving skills, and life-long learning habits.

Getting started

You can start out in industrial electronics in product assembly. You can begin this kind of job without specialized training. Sometimes, you can use your on-the-job experience to earn a promotion to frontline supervisor or production manager. Some companies might require experience and further education for these jobs. If you are interested in engineering, such as designing products, production methods, or robots to do production jobs, the more hand-on experience you can get, the better you'll do your job. Working in assembly while you are in school would be a valuable part of your education. And you'll get paid for learning.

Things you can do to get a head start

A high school degree or equivalency diploma is required for most assembly jobs. Two-year college and technical degrees can qualify you for technician's jobs, assisting in the production planning and design processes. More responsibility in directing the processes requires a 4-year degree. Many engineers seek advanced graduate degrees. This may be necessary for engineering management or new product development.

Designing robotics nearly always means continuing your education after college. There are a lot of specialties that apply. Engineering, physics, computer science, and mathematics degrees can all be part of robotics. Technicians assist in these areas also.

Regardless of where you might want to work in industrial electronics or robotry, you will have to understand processes. Building a product and building a robot both involve understanding the steps necessary to accomplish complex tasks, breaking the steps down into small parts and designing processes to complete the job in the most cost-efficient, safe, and high-quality manner available.

Let's Meet...

Bill Flynn
Production Supervisor

Bill is a frontline supervisor. There are 31 assembly workers in his unit. He makes sure that the electronic equipment they produce is made on time and in keeping with highest safety and quality standards.

What qualities make you successful in the job?

The key aspect to my success is trust in people. I've found that people do their best work when they do it on their own, without having a supervisor "breathe down their necks." When they are trusted to do their best, they do. It makes for a better working life for all of us.

What do you like most about your job?

Our products—respirators—dramatically improve people's lives. So, customer satisfaction is certainly the most rewarding aspect of the job. Getting a quality product to people who need it when they need it and knowing or finding out how it has changed their lives for the better is exhilarating. I also love seeing the people who work here learn new skills and take pride in turning out a high-quality product.

What are your favorite activities on the job?

I can summarize that with three words: coach, counsel, and motivate. My job is working with people not machinery or products. I have to be very sensitive to the people I work with and deal with the whole person. I help them build up their skills, confidence, and pride in their work.

What is the biggest problem that you have had to solve?

One of the assemblers in the unit found that the switch on a new product wasn't working correctly. It showed how good our workers are. All he saw was a split-second flash in the testing process. But, if he hadn't caught it, the products would have been defective. The units would have been recalled. This saved the company money and pride.

Describe your work environment.

First of all, it's extraordinarily clean and quiet for an assembly plant. The cleanliness is because of the nature of the product. Where noisy tools are used, the noise is muffled by a plastic tent that covers that work area. A similar tent with a vent is used to keep fumes from glues and other chemicals out of the factory air.

There is stress involved in making sure that a certain number of units are produced on time. I try to keep this stress from bothering the assemblers. I don't want them to feel that they have to rush. This could endanger the quality of the product.

Safety in the Electronics Shop

Whether working in a home workshop or a large factory, certain safety rules must be followed when working with electronics. Fire and electric shock are constant threats when using electricity improperly.

1. Be sure that all components and materials are properly insulated. Replace any frayed or worn cords as soon as possible. Electrician's tape is a quick but temporary fix. Noninsulating tape should never be used.

2. Your equipment must also be grounded. Most cords have special polarized plugs that ensure grounding when properly inserted. Always use polarized extension cords and receptacles. If you use an adapter, be sure to connect the grounding wire from the adapter to the center screw of the wall plate.

3. Static electricity from your body is another danger. If you do not have a metallic grounding "bracelet" or wrist strap, be sure to discharge any static buildup regularly by moving away from the work area.

4. Be sure that your circuit breaker or fuse is the appropriate rating. It protects you from too much current passing through the components. When a fuse blows out or a circuit breaker breaks, replace or reset it. If it occurs over and over, something is wrong. You will need to call in a qualified electrician. Never bypass the fuse. It is your protection.

5. Don't overload your wall sockets with extensions or cube plugs. This risks fire. Instead, use a power strip. They have built-in fuses for protection from overloading.

Let's Meet...

Lin Chase
Robot Designer

Lin talks to her robot, Alphie. And Alphie talks back. Alphie helps children and adults learn to read. It shows them a passage and listens carefully as they read it. Alphie is a new kind of robot.

How did you become interested in robotics?

I've always been interested in the combination of people and computers. Building a computer requires you to understand people better. I've also studied languages. Right now, I'm learning Japanese. Creating robots that use language combines my loves of people, languages, and technology. Someday, my grandchildren will say to me, "I can't believe that you had to *type* into a computer."

What career path have you followed?

I studied physics and did research in computer science on "artificial intelligence" while I was in college. Then, I worked for about 6 years in industry writing computer programs to make factories work "smarter." This is called "artificial intelligence," because it tries to make computers think like people do. I continued study in graduate school and decided to specialize in speech recognition, which is a kind of artificial intelligence.

What has been your toughest problem on the job?

It has been a personal, not technical problem. There are still not many women in robotics. Sometimes the job can be very lonely. I find myself being the one who cares about the technical problem we are tackling and how the team works together to tackle it. But, I do notice that more men are paying attention to the people side of things and how it can make solving the technical problems easier.

What are the qualities that make you successful in this job?

I am very tenacious and will stick and stick to something until I get it done. You have to go over your work and try it over again and again. You have to be tremendously patient, attending to every detail as though it was the most important part of the project. Robots do not think for themselves. They have no common sense or intuition to make up for their mistakes as a human worker would. Any small thing can stop the whole process.

What will you be doing 5 years from now?

I see a future in developing robotics to solve practical problems that will help people work and learn better. There are infinite possibilities in the future of robotics. You are only limited by your talent and determination.

Reading the "Mind" of a Robot

Where people have neurons and electric impulses, robots have chips and electronic impulses.

From the time you are born, people talk and make baby sounds for you to hear. The sounds are coded in your memory as you hear the sounds over and over. People from different countries, or different areas of a country, hear different sounds. This is how we acquire an accent.

The robot gets training in an *acoustic model*. All of the sounds that comprise the language are programmed into the computer by repetition. The robot "hears" a lot of different people and can understand slight differences in speech.

The robot is not as good as you are though, at figuring out what a person has said when it didn't quite hear all the words. And robots can't read lips to help them either!

Many people talk and read to you as you grow up. You get used to sounds that go together and you recognize the patterns as words. You learn patterns for putting the words together in sentences. The robot gets trained in a *language model* by being read to over and over and over by many different people.

You learn the meanings of the words. People show you and tell you what they mean as they talk to you. The robot has a *dictionary* programmed directly into its memory. Then, it can give the patterns of words meaning.

When the robot hears sounds, they are converted first to electronic current, then to a digital representation. When the robot talks back, the digital representations are transformed to current, then to speech or typewritten words.

Success Stories

Nolan Kay Bushnell, founder of Atari and Pizza Time restaurants, was a pioneer among product engineers. In 1972 he founded Atari, a leader in developing unique electronic products for home entertainment. Atari was very successful, stirring up and riding the huge wave of interest in video games. After selling Atari, Bushnell went on to pioneer in robotry, of sorts, using the famous "pizza" robots in his new venture "Pizza Time Theater" Restaurants. Nolan was a better engineer than restaurateur, and Pizza Time, less successful than Atari, went bankrupt. But, the "pizza" robots who entertained the customers will be fondly remembered by many for a long time.

Working with the idea that robots do well what is dangerous for humans, Christy A. Peake founded companies to design, develop, and build robots for use in the military and in the security business. Her companies are Fared Robot Systems and Robot Defense Systems. One of her first models, the Prowler looks like a tank. Instead of holding persons inside who control it, the Prowler can be controlled via radio waves, by electronic messages that pass from a control unit through wires or by an on-board computer. This takes humans out of the danger zone. The Prowler can perform surveillance, rescue, and other missions.

Find Out More

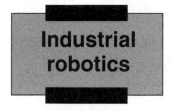

Industrial robotics

Analyze the process for completing a simple task like tying a shoe or screwing the lid onto a jar. Now write step-by-step directions for completing the task successfully. Have a friend act like a robot and follow your directions exactly. How well did he or she complete the task?

If your robot completed the task successfully, CONGRATULATIONS! You have potential as a robotics engineer. If the task wasn't completed correctly, analyze the process. Did your robot make any errors in following the directions exactly?

Were your directions complete and correct?

Try again and see if your robot can accomplish its mission.

Find out more about electronics assembly

To find out more about electronics assembly, you might want to start building your own electronic equipment. Many electronics and hobby stores sell kits to make radios, calculators, and other equipment.

Institute of Industrial Engineers
25 Technology Park/Atlanta
Norcross, GA 30092

The Robotics Institute
4910 Forbes Ave.
Carnegie Mellon University
Pittsburgh, PA 15213-3890

Institute of Electrical and
    Electronics Engineers
345 E. 47th St.
New York, NY 10017

ELECTRONICS IN CARS, BUSES, AND TRAINS

W e are all in a hurry to get where we are going, fast and then faster yet. The greater the speed, the greater the need for control. Better and faster controls means more reliable, more efficient, more responsive information systems. Speed, information, and control are the hallmarks of high performance electronics. Information must move faster than the vehicle it must control, whether that vehicle is a passenger car, a bus, a subway train, or a freight train. Electronics helps make all of this possible.

What it's like to work in ground transportation

Automotive manufacturers have recently been modernizing and updating their manufacturing plants to make the most of the workers' skills and talents. Workers are organized into teams with more flexibility in their job duties and more responsibility for decision making about their jobs.

Railroads have also modernized. They are changing to make train travel more pleasant and appealing. This improves working conditions in the industry also. Cleaner conditions prevail throughout the industry.

Working in assembly, for subway systems and many railroad jobs, requires working in shifts, with some nighttime and weekend work. Service, or mechanics', work has the advantage of more regular hours, although some evenings and weekends may be required.

The importance of electronics in cars, buses, and trains

Every year, car buyers look for increased safety and performance. The automotive industry depends on automotive technology to improve the design of car systems and sell its cars. People want cars that accelerate faster, brake smoothly, and hold the road. Electronic sensors make these improvements possible. They continuously collect data about road and driving conditions. The data is fed into on-board computers. The computers control the car and respond as needed to maintain safety. These electronic systems respond faster than many drivers could, taking over some of the driver's job. Electronic technology is so far advanced that cars that steer themselves are already on the horizon.

Mass transit systems have also grown more complex. The increasing size and number of buses on the road call for sophisticated controls and communications. This has meant developing and installing better electronic systems.

Technology has also pushed light rail and train transportation forward. Subways and light rail transit trains are controlled from central locations. Complex electronic systems keep them on track and on time. This can even occur without a human conductor on board.

The importance of ground transportation electronics

The transportation industry is one of the largest U.S. employers. Hundreds of thousands of people are employed making cars, trucks, and buses. Hundreds of thousands more are employed indirectly, manufacturing, servicing, and operating electronic components. Whether you want to work for one of the largest companies in the world—the automobile manufacturers—or the smallest—

your own service station—there
are opportunities for growth in
applying electronics skills to
ground transportation.

There has been one striking
trend in employment figures for
the industry. Demand for
unskilled or semiskilled workers
is decreasing. Demand for skilled
workers, particularly in electronics, is increasing.

Very skilled design engineers
and technicians build the electronic circuits that keep the
industry up-to-date and competi-
tive. Skilled production workers,
who can adapt to changing job
tasks and can build complex systems, are needed in assembly.

The same is true in service.
Increases in the number of cars
on the road will keep service technicians employed. The skill level
required for these positions is
increasing. Many car dealers and
manufacturers are having a hard
time finding as many qualified
mechanics as they need.

Getting started

Starting in service or assembly
requires a high school degree.
Technical training helps to get a
job. A 2-year technical degree or
some coursework after high school
gives you an advantage in getting
a job and in advancing more
quickly.

Entry-level jobs assisting in
transportation research or design

require the technical degree or years of job experience. Engineers and scientists are in charge of the research and development. As for any electronics job, good preparation in mathematics and science is of real benefit. Mechanical skills are needed at every level, for assembling equipment in production, to disassembling and reassembling it in testing and service.

Technical writers who understand electronics work can translate the technical language of the engineers into owners' manuals that the general public can understand. They may have communication or technical degrees.

The rewards, the pay, and the perks

Automotive workers are among the best paid and have some of the best benefits in business. Railroad workers also receive good benefits and wages. Bus and light rail workers usually work for local transit authorities. In most cases these jobs are controlled by union rules and wage schedules. On-the-job training is continuously provided by most manufacturers, transportation companies, and service stations. Most also pay for courses that increase workers' skills.

Let's Meet...

Don Graham
Automotive Journeyman and Master Mechanic

About 60 to 80 percent of a car is run by electronics. Passenger cars can easily have 10 computers on board. Specialized training in electronics is very important for Don to do his job successfully.

How did you become interested in electronics?

I spent a lot of time taking things apart when I was a kid. I was always especially interested in electronic and mechanical things. My interests in cars and electronics grew hand in hand. It's fascinating to figure out how things work, why they break, and how to fix them so that they won't break again.

What specialized training do you need to start out?

Most states require automobiles to be inspected for safety and pollution control. The licenses for doing these inspections are the basic qualifications an employer would look for. Some employers will hire you without the licenses, if they think you'll make a good mechanic. They may give you on-the-job training and pay for you to take the tests.

What has been your career path?

I started college in electrical engineering. But I decided I wanted something more active and physical. I started as a lot attendant, washing cars, and moved up to rust proofing and other less-technical jobs. After I got my licenses, I was hired as an apprentice mechanic. Since then, I've continued training, completing all of the American Service Excellence certifications, and am at the highest level—a journeyman.

What do you like most about the job?

I like the diversity. You never do the same thing day after day. You have different cars with different problems to fix every day. You also have to think. Electronics is not an exact science. You may fix one part, but still find that the problem isn't fixed. You have to dig deeper to find the solution.

Are there any drawbacks to the job?

It's very physically demanding at times. And it's frustrating when you have a hard time getting to the bottom of a problem. There is also a lot of paperwork that isn't much fun.

What qualities do you need to do your job successfully?

The most important is being conscientious. That means getting to the root of the problem. We call some mechanics "parts heads." If a part is broken, they just replace it. But, that's not doing the job. Whatever caused the part to break will usually cause it to break again. You need to find out why it broke and fix that.

Testing and Wiring

Electronic technicians working in maintenance and service test parts to help them find problems. They also have to repair and rewire circuitry. Following these simple instructions, you can test batteries in your house and build simple circuits.

Supplies
1.5-volt batteries
thin gauge wire
flashlight bulb

—Contact

Contact——

A Simple Tester
Begin by building a simple circuit. Be sure that the power source is connected from its poles to the contact points on the bulb to complete the circuit.

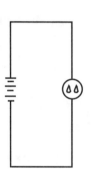

You can test all of the 1.5-volt batteries in your house using this simple testing device.

SAFETY TIPS

1. Use only 1.5-volt batteries. The value of these batteries is not enough to shock you. Do not use higher value batteries or house current from wall receptacles.
2. Use electrical tape to make your connections. Even though you are using low value batteries, practice safety at all times. Keep the insulating materials on your wires, stripping only the point of contact.
3. You can use twist ties that come from bread wrappers or plastic bags for wiring in these experiments. Even though the current value is weak (You could hold the connections with your fingers and not receive a shock.), insulate the wires with electrical tape.

Let's Meet...

Edie Murphy
Radio Communications Technician

Edie services and repairs the electronic radio communication, public address, and sign systems on the buses of a large city.

How did you become interested in electronics?

After high school, I realized that I needed more knowledge and skills to make something of myself. I wanted more out of life than I could get with my diploma. I chose electronics. The program qualified me to go into many areas of electronics and opened up a lot of good job possibilities. I learned that there are jobs out there, if you are willing to pursue the goal.

What special certifications or training do you have?

I completed a program in basic and advanced electronics and an additional 6 months of robotics. I could have entered many areas of electronics. To repair and work on communication equipment I had to get an FCC (Federal Communications Commission) license by passing a written exam.

Have you had further training after getting your job?

Yes. We are constantly being schooled on new equipment systems or take refresher courses.

What is your typical day like?

The workday is from 8 A.M. to 4:30 P.M., Monday through Friday. Each morning, I get a list from my supervisor that says what repairs need to be done to each bus in the shop. I am the only communications technician in this garage. I remove faulty equipment and replace it with new or repaired equipment. This gets the buses back on schedule in the fastest manner. When the buses are ready, I fix the equipment that I replaced so it can be put into another bus when needed.

What are your favorite activities on the job?

I like trouble shooting, repairing equipment, regardless of which type it is. I like figuring out the problem that caused the equipment to go bad and then solving it. I also enjoy the physical activities like soldering the circuits and rewiring. I enjoy the responsibility of working by myself and seeing that I've done a good job. There really isn't anything that I don't like about this job.

What are your plans for future career moves?

I enjoy working with my hands and solving problems. After my family is raised, I would like to establish my own business selling or servicing electronic equipment.

Studying the Want Ads

This book introduces you to some of the many kinds of jobs found in the electronics field. Another good way to learn about the kinds of jobs available and the qualifications needed for them are the classified advertisements of the Sunday paper. Make a listing of the jobs that you find advertised and the information that you can discover. All newspapers have different formats, but the following chart can serve as a guide.

To start your search, check to see if there is a "Technical" section in the want ads. If there is, check there first. If not, check under the "E" for electronics, "T" for technician, "A" for assembly, and so on. Health care, sales, and computer sections are other good possibilities.

	# of Jobs	Ranges: Qualifications	Salary	Benefits
Electronics Assembly				
Electronics Technicians				
Electronics Engineers				

Not all of the information will be listed for each job. But, you can get an idea. If any look particularly interesting, you might want to call the employer to find out more details about the job and the kind of person he or she is looking for.

Success Stories

Thomas Zimmerman is an automotive engineer who is putting radar in cars. An antenna in the taillight or on the outside rearview mirror sends data to a computer control that could make "intelligent" decisions about safe driving. It sends the distance between the car and vehicles in front or behind it and, through a computer, adjusts the cruise control speed to maintain safe distances. Currently cruise control maintains a constant speed, regardless of the speed or distance of other vehicles. This "intelligent" cruise control increases safety. The radar detects potential hazards forward, backward, and in changing lanes.

Kathleen M. Hammer is an automotive product design engineer. She develops state-of-the-art, high-resolution electron spectrometry and nuclear magnetic resonance imaging for use in dashboard display. Her electronics ensure that drivers get precise information as they need it and in a form that is easily read. Her digital speedometer and graphic displays are used in the latest model vehicles. These systems, that can be read from various angles, depending on the height of the driver's head and in varying light conditions, require sophisticated electronic technology.

Find Out More

You and car, bus, and train electronics

Automobile dealers are found in every city. Ask if you can visit a repair shop to get a look under the hood of a car. Where are the electronics located? What systems of the car do they operate? They may also tell you about finding a job with automobile manufacturers.

Ask for booklets about new cars. Usually these will advertise the technological advances of the newest models and their electronics systems.

There are still about 500 railroad companies operating in the United States. Most large cities have offices of one or two of the major companies. Their public relations or human resource departments can provide information about the kinds of jobs available at different locations.

Subway and bus systems are operated by the local public transit authority. Their offices are listed in your telephone book. They can provide employment and general information.

Find out more about ground transportation electronics

Office of Information and Public
   Affairs
Association of American Railroads
Library Room 5800
50 F St., N.W.
Washington, DC 20001

National Association for
   Automotive Service Excellence
Suite 400
1920 Association Dr.
Reston, VA 22091

Automotive Service Industry
   Association
444 N. Michigan Ave.
Chicago, IL 60611

ELECTRONICS IN COMMUNICATION AND AT HOME

E very area of electronic technology is a fast-paced field of dynamic growth and potential. But broadcast communication may be the area with the most revolutionary power. A twist of a satellite dish can transport a 10-year old in the mountains of West Virginia and another in a high rise in New York City to an African rain forest. It can take them anywhere on the globe.

Our homes are filled with electronics. This includes radio, television, telephone, audio tape, videotape, computer transmissions, calculators, video games, microwave ovens, and garage door openers. All are information exchanges through circuitry.

What it's like to work in home electronics and communications

Broadcast and consumer electronics offer jobs for a wide range of educational levels and interests. Operators, technicians, engineers, manufacturing, and sales all play important roles. Operators work strictly with the equipment, while technicians are expected to be able to repair or assist in engineering tasks. In broadcast, many technicians have specialties, such as lighting, sound, video, and transmission. Engineers design products and processes to produce them.

The business end covers product development, coming up with new ideas for products and new uses and users for old products, sales, and repair shops. One salesperson might be calling on companies and industries, convincing them to install his or her telephones, computer network, video cameras, and screens for security or other large-scale sales. Another salesperson will work in a store and have to be well informed on many kinds of telephones, computers, televisions, video cameras, radios, etc. in order to advise customers on the best one. Service and repair technicians work for large and small companies or open their own repair shop.

Working conditions will vary according to the type of industry in which you are employed. Radio or television stations are comfortable surroundings. Repair technicians may find themselves outdoors in any type of weather on lines or satellite dishes.

Communication goes on around the clock. Radio and television stations often work 24 hours a day, 7 days a week, and especially on holidays. Stores and repair shops need to be open when customers can come in. Nearly everyone in communication and consumer electronics can expect, at least at one point in his or her career, to work evening, weekend, or nighttime shifts.

The future of broadcast and consumer electronics

People with business and technical knowledge will be in demand as communication and consumer electronics continues to grow and grow. The newest among the consumer products combine forms to bring us the magic of interactive programming through computers and phone lines using television as the end display device. In the arts, electronics brings the fingertips of a pianist in Paris to depress the keys of a piano in a concert hall in New York. Two dancers' images appear on-screen, one is dancing in London, one in Tokyo.

Fiber optics is about to revolutionize communication again. Its main advantage is speed. Electronic circuitry is fast. But fast depends on the speed of electrons. Fiber optics will travel at the speed of light.

The rewards, the pay, and the perks

Many of the jobs in communication as operators or technicians pay hourly wages. Pay can range widely, usually the larger the station is, the more it will pay. Salespeople are usually paid an hourly or monthly base salary, which is a minimum. They also get a commission, which means that the more you sell, the more money you make.

For those who like to travel, selling large communication systems and equipment can take you on the road most days of the week. Operators and technicians have little travel, unless they work for the military. Servicing and repairing equipment takes you traveling wherever your customers are. This could be around the world if you sell very specialized equipment like communication satellites, air traffic communications, or police radar equipment. You might need to travel around the corner if you repair televisions or home video equipment.

Things you can do now

• Take a room-by-room survey of your house. How many devices are controlled by electronics? How would your day-to-day life be different without them? Now, visit an electronics store or browse a store catalog or advertising brochure. How many more products can you find?

- A local electronics repair shop may be willing to have eager students spend time learning firsthand about the trade. Some may even be interested in having a young apprentice to help them out on Saturdays or during the summer.

- Retired and small business operators are often willing to share their knowledge. Call your local Small Business Association, Chamber of Commerce or American Association of Retired Persons (AARP) to see if they have a listing of service shopowners who have volunteered to share their experience.

- Television and radio stations are eager to have larger audiences. Both cable and network stations produce programming and receive it from satellites circling high above the earth. Contact their public relations offices for tours of their studios and satellite facilities or for a speaker to come to your school or club.

Let's Meet...

Paula Roemele
Broadcast Technician

Paula's transmission board is the last stop for television signals at WPXI TV station. She has to be sure that all of the programming is transmitted in high-quality audio and video, timed exactly, in the proper sequence.

How did you become interested in a career in broadcast?

While I was in school I worked as a receptionist in a recording studio. I was bit by the entertainment bug. My next step was to volunteer to work part time at a television station. I impressed them with my enthusiasm and willingness to work hard. They hired me and I worked part time there until I finished school.

What activities are involved in your job?

Everything that goes on our channel on the TV screen passes through my transmission board. I have to monitor and adjust the quality of the video and audio broadcasts. I have to follow the schedule and see that everything gets broadcast in the right sequence and for the right amount of time. I have to coordinate taped and live programs and local and network programming. I have to keep a record of everything and maintain the library of tapes.

What special training have you had?

Most of my training has been on-the-job training. I was the first woman to work in the newsroom, as a weekend assignment editor and occasional writer. To become a technician, I had to complete courses, for which the station paid, in electronics.

What qualities have made you successful in your work?

Willingness to accept responsibility is critical. Technicians used to be expected to just follow orders, not think for themselves. This has never been part of my nature, but now the job expectations have changed. Now it is expected that the technicians will do a lot of on-the-spot decision making.

What accomplishments are you most proud of?

I have been able to bridge the communication gap between the engineering department and the rest of the building. The language of the department can be highly technical. This makes me a problem solver in the department.

What are the hardest aspects of the job?

The job is not physically hard or technically hard. I've been in this job for 17 years and for the first years it was hard to communicate. I had to learn a whole new technical language.

Watching TV with a Transmission Technician's Eye

The next time you watch television or listen to the radio, make notes of how many times the programming changes in one half-hour. Count each different commercial, each program segment, each announcement as a change. It is for Paula, because each change means a different tape had to be loaded and programmed to start.

	Program Segments	Announcements	Commercials
Number of Times/Duration			

Note any errors. Was there any empty space when the screen went black or filled with static? Did a commercial run twice in a row? Was the audio or video segment of poor quality or mismatched? These mistakes may be unusual, but they all can happen. When we look for them, we may notice a lot.

	Empty Space	Audio Error	Video Error	Other
Number of Times/Duration				

Practice Programming

You are responsible for scheduling programming for one evening. The time slot runs from 6 P.M. to 11 P.M. You need to fill it with 6 to 10 programs, commercials, and public service announcements. Fit them into the schedule in a way that you think will attract and keep viewers. How good of a job did you do?

Let's Meet...

Howard Jefferson
District Manager, Retail Sales

Howard supervises 25 stores with 110 employees. He is responsible for hiring, training, and supervising the salespeople, store managers, and manager trainees. His hobby led to this career.

How did you get interested in this field?

I like gadgets. In high school I ran things like the public address board and radio room. I've always enjoyed electronics.

What has been your career path to becoming district manager?

While in high school, I worked in a pet shop. I found out that I had a real gift for relating to people and finding the right pet for them. I was able to work my way up from sales to becoming store manager.

When did you combine your love of electronics and sales?

I was spending most of my money at the electronics shop. When the pet shop was sold, I entered the manager training program here. I was able to combine my hobby and my job.

Did you have any special training?

I learned electronics on my own, through my hobbies. As a

manager trainee, I had on-the-job training. I learned by observing the manager. I learned by not being afraid to ask questions. By knowing who knew the answer to a question I had and asking them.

What do you like most about your work?

I like seeing the people that I hired and trained become successful. I like really digging in and helping them. I like people liking me and needing my help. I also love being able to work with the things, the electronics, that I like to play with.

What are your strengths?

Getting involved is one. If I see something that needs to be done, I get in and do it. Many managers like acting "like executives," telling people what to do. I'd rather coach them, help them figure it out for themselves.

Also, I never forget where I came from. I know what it's like to be a salesperson and a store manager. I know what they are up against, what they face everyday.

What are your least favorite parts of the job?

I hate to see people quit and give up. Some younger adults want to get to the top of the ladder right away. They may be willing to do the work, but not put in the years it takes to move up through the ranks. It takes patience.

Two Challenges from Howard

Improving a Product

Take an inventory of all of the electronic devices in your house. Can you think of a way that each of them could be improved? That is the job of the engineers and businesspersons who work in product development. A good salesperson is also alert to customer's needs and working with developers to meet them.

Creating New Products or New Markets

Can you think of a job that needs to be done better in your home or classroom. Do you think that you could come up with ideas for electronic products that could do the job? Consider all the details ... what would the device have to do? Create a product to meet a need ... find uses for a new product ... find new users for an old product ... explain the benefits.

Success Stories

Rising to the top of one's profession is an accomplishment that many people strive for. Rising to the top of two professions is an accomplishment that few of us would even dream of, but Arthur C. Clarke has achieved that as a scientist and science fiction writer. As a mathematician and physicist, Clarke invented the geosynchronous communication satellite in 1945. It became a reality in 1967 as Telstar. For it, he won prestigious awards of the scientific community: a Marconi International Fellowship; a gold medal of the Franklin Institute; a fellowship of King's College, London; and the Vikram Sarabhai Professorship of the Physical Research Laboratory, Ahmedabad, India.

Clarke has also written more than 50 science and science fiction books, and won many literary awards. Not stopping with the print media, Clarke wrote a screenplay from one of his outstanding novels, *2001: A Space Odyssey*. He covered hard news with Walter Cronkite for CBS during the Apollo moon missions, and he had his own television series.

 In the 1950s the world was still figuring how best to use the broadcast media. At WQED in Pittsburgh, the nation's first public television station, Josie Carey was making history in programming for children. Working against a canvas background for 7 years, she and Fred Rogers broadcast "Children's Corner." Ad-libbing with puppets, for which Mr. Rogers supplied the voices, and writing songs, she entranced and educated thousands of children in 26 states through the 50s. Their show received many awards, including the Sylvania, which was the forerunner of the Emmy.

After a full career in television, Ms. Carey is now writing and directing "Trivia: the Musical" for the college stage. In 1994, October 12 was proclaimed "Josie Carey Day" in Pittsburgh in celebration of her 40th anniversary in broadcasting.

Find Out More

Find out more about electronics in communication and at home

Learn more about electronics in communication and at home by contacting these organizations:

National Association of
    Broadcasters
1771 N St., N.W.
Washington, DC 20036

National Electronic Sales and
    Service Dealers Association
2708 W. Berry St.
Fort Worth, TX 76109

National Cable Television
    Association
1724 Massachusetts Ave., N.W.
Washington, DC 20036

Federal Communications
    Commission
1919 M St., N.W.
Washington, DC 20554

ELECTRONICS IN AEROSPACE

D aily, thousands of people flying in commercial and private planes depend on the reliability of air and space electronics, also called avionics. The security of pilots in training or in battle and of astronauts in space depend on this technology. It is very sophisticated and heavily researched and tested. Developments in the aerospace industry, particularly in military development and the space program, have propelled technological advances in other specialties. Night vision glasses, global positioning, even microwave ovens—all began as inventions of air and space electronics.

Electronics has helped us rendezvous spacecraft thousands of miles from earth, land Americans on the moon, and shuttle astronauts and scientists around in space routinely. It has also made possible unmanned missions to distant planets, satellites circling the earth, and, missiles and rockets of every sort. It has advanced science, communication, defense, and entertainment.

Aviation began with the 1903 flight of the Wright brothers in Kitty Hawk, North Carolina. In the 90 years since then, aerospace technology has crossed the Atlantic Ocean in 4 hours, circled the earth, and traveled to the moon and Mars. Power and physics provided the keys for the first series of advances. Aviation electronics is the key to newest developments. An advanced plane or spaceship without electronics is like a body without a brain or nervous system. It is full of potential but unable to use it wisely.

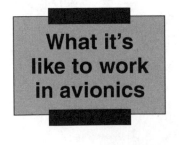

What it's like to work in avionics

Electronics scientists, engineers, and technicians who work on air and space systems work for airlines, the government, and for companies that build planes and spacecraft or the electronic systems that go in them. In the government, they work for the military and the National Aeronautics and Space Administration (NASA). There are jobs in research and production for engineers, scientists, and technicians in government and industry.

The airlines employ most of the "hands-on" people. Electronics technicians are mechanics, quality control experts, and flight engineers. They are responsible for instruments before a flight, continuous monitoring during the flight, and checks after the flight. They ensure that all necessary repairs and adjustments are done.

The pleasures and pressures of the job

The demands for safety and reliability in the aerospace industry are higher than in any other field of electronics. The work force is the most highly skilled and trained in electronics. In many other industries, up to two-thirds of the jobs may be at the lower skill and training levels. In the aerospace industry, though, the demand for highly skilled technicians and engineers is growing, but the demand for unskilled or semiskilled labor is shrinking.

Being able to communicate orally and in writing is extremely important. Engineers have to sell their ideas and their ability to make their ideas realities. A lot of scientific and report writing is done, so that others may test and verify their work.

Most technicians and engineers become specialists in a particular field, such as communication, navigation, guidance, display systems, infrared technology, or radar detection. Most people begin their specialization after they are hired through on-the-job training and working with experts already in the field.

You have to be a problem solver. You need to be able to find new ways to look at a problem and to find new and workable solutions. Aerospace needs push technology to its edge. Being successful means pushing far past not only what has been done but what has been dreamed.

Climbing the career ladder

Moving into management requires a new set of skills. Most managers, from mid level up to the chief officers, are scientists and engineers. They rise in management as they take on more and more responsibility for supervising the work of others and as their projects grow larger. Managers need to be experts. They have to have a body of experience that includes knowing the technology and the other experts so they can continue to build, not repeat.

A few scientists and engineers are able to keep research and product development as their primary focus. These top-ranking researchers are called "senior engineers" or "distinguished fellows." Their salaries are equal to those of high-level management.

Technicians also advance through levels of increasing responsibility. Nearly all work as apprentices, until they are expert in their specialization. They can then advance to supervising other technicians. Another path to advancement is moving from testing and repairing into installation, training, or research.

The rewards, the pay, and the perks

The pay scales are higher than in most other areas of production.

The need for avionics to advance, to develop faster, safer, and more accurate systems, requires everyone to be a lifelong learner. Even an engineering degree is a "learner's permit" in avionics. Most companies reimburse employees, directly or through promotions and pay increases, for continuing their studies throughout their careers. Most companies provide opportunities for on-the-job training in new skill areas, to keep their work force flexible to meet new challenges and opportunities.

Let's Meet...

Gene Adam
Electronics Engineer

Gene is a systems engineer. He imagines, designs, and develops electronic dream machines that give pilots the information they need to fly safely whether in combat or commercial flight.

How did you discover avionics?

After high school, I joined the Navy and was sent to electronics school. I also became a pilot. I learned how tricky it is to maneuver a plane in battle, how electronics works, and how important it is to flying and fighting.

Why did you specialize in display systems?

One of the most important things for a combat pilot is awareness of everything going on in the area. The more information pilots have, the quicker they have it and can respond to it, the more control they have over their situation. Our fighter pilots needed better cockpit displays. I had experience flying and fighting, so I knew what was needed.

What qualities, aside from knowledge, do you need to do your job well?

You have to be patient. In commercial production it may only take 12 months from idea to finished product. Often in military production, it can take 12 years.

You have to have a "salesman's sense" about you. You have to be good with words to sell a new product idea to the people who will pay for it and those who will finally use it.

What are the rewards in doing your work?

There are many personal rewards. Every advance is a new first. Now planes are multipurpose. They can respond to either ground or air threats. A single strike fighter, crewed by only the pilot, has replaced two planes and three people. This means that fewer people are put over enemy territory in any mission. It also saves taxpayers millions and millions of dollars.

Each new design gives the pilot more control over his or her situation. I take pride in making our pilots like "King Kong" by giving them a superior weapon.

What are the toughest problems you have encountered?

There are two types of problems: technical and psychological. If you have found the best that a technology can do, but it isn't good enough, you have to rethink it, come up with a totally different angle.

The psychological problems are trying to convince people that new ways of doing things are possible. This is particularly true with pilots. It can be tough to sell them on a new technology. Their lives depend on their equipment. If they trust it, they don't want to give it up.

Cockpit Designs: Then and Now

In these pictures you can see the evolution of the cockpit designs Gene has developed, from the F-4 fighter plane to the newest prototype plane. Look at the difference it makes for the pilot!

Let's Meet...

Ann Pesta
Automatic Guidance and Control Systems Technician

Ann maintains and repairs automatic pilot and control systems of planes in the U.S. Air Force. She is in the Air Force Reserves.

What kind of training and qualities do you need to be a successful avionics technician?

For the entry-level job, I went to Air Force Technical School for 6 months. To advance, I took correspondence courses. With experience, I reached the technician position. I also have degrees in avionics and biomedical equipment.

As far as qualities are concerned, you must be very organized, conscientious, and have a "can-do" attitude. I am willing to do whatever it takes to get the job done. If you don't know how to solve a problem, you must be willing to ask for help.

What are your favorite parts of the job?

I love using my hands and my brain to fix the equipment on the planes. It gives me a chance to use my skills to my best ability and, most importantly, know that I've done my job efficiently and safely. People's lives depend on

me doing my job precisely. I enjoy the responsibility. It's a little scary, but very exciting.

What are some of the other benefits of the job?

Travel is one. We do duties on other bases, in the United States and in other countries. I've been through Europe and to Panama several times. The Air Force invests a lot of money in our education. That saves me a lot of money. They also provide us with opportunities to keep our skills up-to-date. When we travel to other bases, we work on different types of planes. There is continuous training to keep up with the new technologies. With every piece of new equipment we have to relearn parts of our job. The Air Force provides career development courses for this.

What accomplishments are you most proud of?

I have received the "Airman of the Month" award. The unit that I work in has achieved many honors. It has been named "Outstanding Unit" many times and has received recognition around the world. I am very happy to be part of a superskilled, competent team. Knowing that you have done your job well is rewarding. You don't always get a pat on the back, but knowing in yourself that you got the plane off the ground safely is something to be very proud of.

Navigation Systems

Finding your way in the dark, on an open lake, or where there are no landmarks, is almost impossible. Modern navigation systems use omnirange transmitters called "omnidomes" to create landmarks for pilots, using radio frequencies. Put yourself in this pilot's plane and find your way safely home.

You have tuned your omnirange receiver into the frequency of two different omnirange transmission stations. Your charts show the locations of all omnirange transmitters. From the radio signals you receive, you can tell your distance from each omnidome.

- Omnirange A's signal indicates that you are 25 miles southeast of it. Omnirange B's signal indicates that you are 20 miles southwest. Using a scale of $1/2$" = 10 miles, find your plane's location on the grid.

- The airport lies beyond the omnidomes. Plot the shortest course to the airport with a dotted line. How far are you from it? (Answers on page 84.)

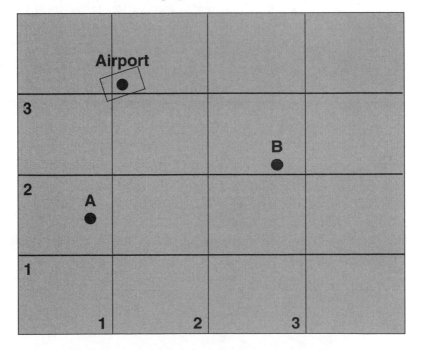

Success Stories

Peggy Dugge

Peggy Dugge has worked on every manned space program from Gemini in the 1960s, including the Apollo moon landings, to the space shuttles. Peggy's calculations helped to be sure that the Gemini spacecraft met at precisely the right spot in infinity. The calculations programmed into the navigation controls of the lunar module ensured that it left the main craft, landed safely, and found its way back to the craft again.

Robert L. Sumpter

Electronics engineer Robert Sumpter led the team that developed the advanced wild weasel during the Vietnam War. At that time pilots in our F-4 fighters averaged only 7 missions. Many people thought that improving the pilots' chances was impossible. But Bob and his team were able to save lives and planes. Moving like cat's ears, the antennae of the advanced wild weasel detect and analyze enemy radar. It transfers the information to a computer that activates a missile or "dump" bomb to destroy the radar. Pilots and planes were freed from the danger of detection. It took 8 years to develop, but is still in use more than 25 years later.

Find Out More

You and avionics

Many airlines give cockpit tours of their planes while they are at the gates or in the hangars between flights. Take a look at the display of electronic equipment bringing information to the pilot and the crew. Can you read the information from the display?

Look under the U.S. Government Offices in your local telephone book for the Federal Aviation Administration. They are responsible for air traffic control at any airport that has air traffic control. You may be able to have a tour of the control tower. Here you'll find electronic equipment busy tracking planes and receiving and sending communications.

Find out more about avionics

National Aeronautics and Space
  Administration (NASA)
300 E St., S.W.
Washington, DC 20546

Flight Engineers International
  Association
906 16th St., N.W.
Washington, DC 20006

Air Transport Association of
  America
1709 New York Ave., N.W.
Washington, DC 20006

Aviation Maintenance
  Foundation, Inc.
P.O. Box 739
Basic, WY 82410

Federal Aviation Administration
Public Inquiry Center
800 Independence Ave., S.W.
Washington, DC 20591

Answers to the puzzle on page 81: Your plane's location is shown by the **X** below. You are 40 miles from the airport.

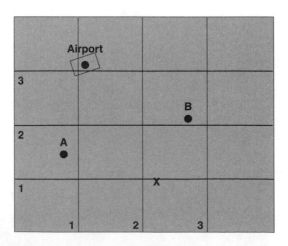

INDEX